HONDA
CB750 FOUR

ROD KER

AMBERLEY

First published 2015

Amberley Publishing
The Hill, Stroud,
Gloucestershire, GL5 4EP

www.amberley-books.com

ISBN: 978 1 4456 5121 7 (print)
ISBN: 978 1 4456 5122 4 (ebook)

British Library Cataloguing in Publication Data.
A catalogue record for this book is available from the British Library.

Typeset in 10pt on 13pt Celeste.
Typesetting by Amberley Publishing.
Printed in the UK.

Contents

Introduction

Thanks to a combination of complacency and naiveté, the traditional European and American motorcycle industry was heading for disaster in the 1960s. In particular, the British were burying their heads deeply in the sand by largely refusing to acknowledge the threat posed by Japanese upstarts. Despite clear evidence that Honda and the other Big Four meant business and were eating into the market, UK manufacturers still served up essentially the same old bikes every year. Primitive production methods, worn-out tooling and the pursuit of speed meant that in many ways typical British bikes were actually worse than they had been in the previous decade.

While Japanese manufacturers were investing in genuinely new designs and modern technology, British boardrooms remained true to the delusion that far eastern factories could only churn out shoddy copies and wouldn't be capable of making large-capacity motorcycles even if they tried.

The first sign that they were totally wrong was the 1965 Honda CB450 twin, which was as fast as most British 650s. Three years later, after persistent rumours that a bigger version of the same thing was about to appear, Honda dropped its four-cylinder bombshell in the form of the CB750, complete with electric starter, five-speed gearbox and front disc brake. More than that, it offered speed, convenience, reliability and oil tightness – features that were normally mutually exclusive.

The first 'superbike' had arrived, and it took the Japanese opposition a long time to catch up.

1

Dreams and Realities

Natural disasters loom large in the life and times of Soichiro Honda. In 1923, the Great Kantō Earthquake destroyed the Tokyo garage where he had worked since leaving school. Honda and another employee rebuilt the business from the ground up, impressing the owner so much that he supported and encouraged young Soichiro in his dream to design and race cars. Evidently, he was equally skilled at driving, and achieved considerable success until suffering a serious accident in 1936. Honda was badly injured but would probably have carried on racing if his family had allowed it.

Instead, he tried something completely different by founding Tokai Seiki Heavy Industry in Hamamatsu, an engineering company manufacturing die-cast piston rings ... At least, it did once Honda had studied metallurgy for long enough to know how it was done! By the end of the decade Toyota was a customer and 40 per cent shareholder, and Tokai Seiki was contributing to the Imperial war effort by producing aircraft parts.

There was little left of Japanese industry once the dust had settled on the Second World War. Hamamatsu was always a prime target for obliteration by US bombers, but in early 1945 another earthquake finished the job. Honda adopted a pragmatic attitude to Japan's ruination and sold his remaining stake in Tokai Seiki in the belief that the company would be split up after the war by the Americans. He must have been devastated by what had happened both to Japan and his former business, but it seems that this was only part of the reason for his next venture.

In 1945, aged nearly forty, Soichiro began a new life basically doing nothing, indulging in what might now be called a gap year. For someone who had worked so hard since leaving school aged sixteen, this 'human holiday' was perhaps an uncharacteristic interlude, but it didn't last long. While his friends and neighbours might have had the impression that Honda's main interest was sitting around making saké, the Japanese version of moonshine, and generally trying to have a good time drinking it every evening, his fertile mind was hatching plans.

Thoughts became action in September 1946 with the appearance of the Honda Technical Research Institute, a rather grand name for what was essentially a glorified garden shed surrounded by a vast wasteland. With around 15 square metres of floor space, there was hardly enough room to swing a cat or a sledgehammer, whichever was the most appropriate for the task in hand.

Initially, HTRI's mission was to make a rotary weaving machine (Hamamatsu was formerly the centre of the Japanese textile industry). However, that proved over-ambitious, and some of the other ideas emerging from the new wooden HQ were even less promising. Nothing if not diverse, these included a salt-making machine, floral frosted glass and roofing sheets made out of woven bamboo set in cement. None of these ever became reality, either because no one (including Honda himself) was particularly interested, or through lack of capital.

Possibly, like all the best ideas, the breakthrough came almost by accident when Honda met up with an old friend and business acquaintance. In the 1930s Kenzaburo Inukai had run a Tokyo taxi company and was a regular client of the garage managed by Honda. Inukai happened to have an army-surplus generator engine, as used to power a military radio set, cluttering up his home. Honda spotted the little two-stroke engine, realising it could be given a new role in a basic motorcycle.

While there would hopefully be little demand for military communications in the future, Japan had a desperate need to mobilise the unemployed masses. Pedal cycles were the traditional and obvious solution, but, despite being five times more efficient than walking, not everyone had the health or inclination to cover more than a few miles.

Mopeds, or 'phut phuts' in Japanese parlance, were hardly an original idea, of course. Pioneering motorcycles of the late nineteenth century were basically pushbikes with an engine slotted into the frame in approximately the same place as the pedalling apparatus. While motorcycle design had advanced greatly by the 1940s, post-war austerity resulted in a return to first principles, inspiring a plethora of motorised bicycles typically propelled by tiny two-stroke engines. An extra half horsepower or so to supplement the human input didn't sound much, but it was enough to make the difference between a sweaty and exhausting trek and a practical journey of perhaps 10 miles.

While scores of similar devices sprang from garden sheds throughout Japan and the West (unscathed America being the one exception), many were badly designed and all too often took more effort to ride than an ordinary bike. The first problem was transferring power from the engine to the wheels. Honda's initial solution involved a friction drive to the front tyre, similar to that adopted by the French Velosolex. While that worked well enough for millions of European customers, the Technical Research Institute chose a more sophisticated belt drive transmission, with the engine bolted inside the diamond frame.

After a period of intense brainstorming and experimentation, by October the first Honda motor bicycle was ready for a road test. Soichiro's no doubt long-suffering wife, Sachi, was volunteered for the task. Apparently, the inaugural outing wasn't a total success, as Mrs H. returned covered in a messy fuel/oil mixture blown back through the carburettor. This was soon sorted out, and the prototype phut phut became a familiar sight around Hamamatsu.

People liked what they saw, so the next stage was a production version. To this end, Honda managed to buy 500 engines from Mikuni. Demonstrating an early commitment to quality control, these were all stripped down, serviced and test ridden before going out to customers who therefore had confidence in the product. As a result, further sales were made chiefly by word of mouth, at the rate of about ten per week.

The man entrusted with quality control was Kiyoshi Kawashima, Honda's first graduate engineer employee who had joined Honda on the understanding that he would have to accept a very low salary. Against a post-war Japanese background of poverty and nine million homeless, he was probably lucky to receive any remuneration – partly because there was as yet no proper banking system, partly because his boss was very lax about keeping the company's accounts up to date! He had far more important things to do.

Inevitably, the next problem was that the supply of army surplus engines ran out, necessitating the bold step of making a replacement from scratch for what would be known as the A-type. With additional finance from Soichiro's father, an unusual 50cc two-stroke took shape with what seemed like a top hat extension of the cylinder barrel. Petrol was in short supply, so it was designed to run on a turpentine fuel made from the sap of pine trees. As a result the new motor belched smoke from its upright cylinder, explaining its 'Chimney' nickname.

This engine fell by the wayside: according to lore it was just too far ahead of its time. Honda designed a more orthodox unit instead. Though sometimes suggested, it wasn't simply a copy of the ex-army unit and featured rotary valve induction rather than simple piston porting. Surprisingly, Honda also wanted to use die-cast components (his piston ring manufacturing background proving useful), resulting in a far more consistent and accurate product. The snag was greatly increased initial cost, but in theory this would be recouped by mass production. In 1947 this was a wildly optimistic possibility because the sums only made sense with thousands of engines, not tens or hundreds, but it showed that Honda was trying to give customers the best, not the cheapest.

By 1948 Soichiro had a viable business that needed better organisation and effective marketing. On 1 September the Honda Motor Co. was incorporated with capital of a million yen, which sounds less impressive when translated into its then sterling equivalent of about £1,000. While not everything progressed entirely smoothly, the appointment of Takeo Fujisawa as managing director put the company on a sound financial footing for a

Model A: the first all-Honda powered two-wheeler. (Honda)

few years and gave Honda the time to do what he did best, design motorcycles – grown-up ones, not primitive phut phuts.

So, the B-type featured an enlarged 89cc engine developing about 3 hp. It also sported three wheels and a large carrying box, plus lighting and front suspension. A step away from mopeds and really a digression from the business in hand. Launched the following year, the D-type, aka Dream, was really the first 100 per cent Honda motorcycle. The engine had been expanded further to 98cc, but it was still a smelly, shrill, unrefined two-stroke. Sales were lower than hoped.

Honda's managing director knew that a four-stroke would open new markets, so chief engineer Kawashima and Honda designed one. As installed in the E-type, the result was an advanced 146cc single with double inlet valves developing 5.5 bhp at 5,000 rpm. The opposition took about ten years to catch up – although in many cases they never did catch up, because the E was the instant success that put Honda on course to become the world's largest motorcycle manufacturer by the end of the 1950s. In the process, most of the hundred-odd rivals existing at the beginning of the decade went out of business or were absorbed. The disappearance of Bridgestone meant that by 1970 there were only three other Japanese manufacturers left: Suzuki, Kawasaki and Yamaha.

Although the new engine was something of a masterpiece, the rest of the chassis was quaint compared to Western efforts, as the president realised when he went on a European tour to see what he was up against. In the Japanese home market the snag was that while the E-type Dream was good, buying one was far beyond the means of most people. Honda therefore took a step back in some ways with the succeeding F-type Cub, which was a moped with a clip-on engine.

The original Dream. Still a two-stroke. (Honda)

Soichiro Honda and Takeo Fujisawa, who looked after the company finances. (Honda)

Apart from being relatively cheap, the F was far superior to the early phut phuts. Cleverly marketed through Japan's network of around 50,000 bicycle dealerships by offering bargain hire purchase terms, production figures soon outstripped those of the Dream, earning Honda a Medal of Honour awarded by the emperor.

Honda Motor Co. continued to expand heading into the 1950s, with a new Tokyo office and about $1 million spent on the latest machine tools. Unfortunately, this coincided with a crisis in the Japanese economy, partly caused by the end of the Korean War and an exodus of relatively rich Americans. Thanks to understanding banks, Honda survived and resumed its upwards trajectory by launching the J-type Benly (from the Japanese 'benri', meaning 'convenience'). Although Soichiro was said to be against copying, he admitted that this one had an engine and pressed steel frame inspired by the German NSU. Ironically, way back in the 1920s, NSU had copied the British Norton single of the era, earning them the unofficial nickname 'Norton Spares Used'! All is fair in motorcycle design?

Although the British deluded themselves that the Japanese would never be able to make large-capacity bikes, the 246cc Dream SA of 1955 proved them wrong. It had a chain-driven overhead camshaft and a strong spine frame. Subsequently enlarged to 350cc, the SB was another wake up call for BSA, Triumph and the rest.

That was only the beginning, as two years later Honda released the quarter-litre C70, a high-revving OHC twin with the potential to produce as much power as pushrod 500s. Although containing more than a hint of NSU, in the near future it would be more likely that everyone else would copy Honda (Laverda's 650/750 twin, for instance). Alas, that

The Cub moped was a step backwards in some ways but proved to be a big seller. (Honda)

wasn't really a possibility for the British without investing in the machinery and tooling required to mass produce parts to such close tolerances.

In 1954 Honda visited the Isle of Man and declared his intention to compete in the TT races. At the time the company had nothing that would have been remotely competitive, so it was a supremely optimistic pledge. No doubt boardrooms all across Europe were echoing with the sound of laughter. As history confirms, no one in the traditional industry should have been even slightly amused. Hondas were at the TT before the end of the decade. The debut with a team of 125s was far from a fairy tale, but within a few years they were winning races in all capacity classes.

The unfeasibly high-revving C70 Dream can be seen as the root of all Honda's later masterworks. Scaled down and enlarged OHC twins followed. In the early 1960s, the pinnacle of the line were the sporty CB92 (125cc) and CB72 (250cc). Though expensive for their capacity (the CB72 was £283 in 1961, when the Triumph Bonneville 650 was listed at £288), in practice they were as fast as much larger machines. The CB92 was credited with 15 bhp at 10,500 rpm and would do over 70 mph, while the 250 gave enough speed to cope with a trip along the new-fangled motorways that had been opening since 1958, maybe clocking the 'ton' in favourable conditions. More than that, the engines thrived on revs, and, despite all the jingoistic scorn heaped upon them from some quarters, Hondas were very reliable. Thanks to precision manufacture and stringent quality control, there was no sense of getting a good or bad bike depending on what day of the week it left the factory.

In the first half of the 1960s European and American manufacturers were still clinging to the idea that the Japanese would only produce small-capacity bikes. That delusion was

Honda quickly out-grew its wooden shed. (Honda)

C92 Benly 125. (Honda)

CB72, 250cc and well worthy of its Super Sports name. (Honda)

CB450, aka 'Black Bomber' – even though it wasn't always black. (Honda)

shattered in 1965 when the CB450 was launched, complete with twin overhead cams and torsion-bar valve springs – features that came directly from the racetracks. The UK price for what became known as the Black Bomber was £360, and it was marketed as a competitor to British 650s like the Triumph Bonneville and BSA A65. That was a tall order, as even with an 8,500 rpm power peak and 12,000 rpm mechanical capability, it gave away at least 5 bhp to the opposition. A Super Sport version was expected but never came. Why it wasn't a full half-litre as per the later CB500T is a mystery, but any lingering doubts about Honda being able to make larger road bikes were dispelled.

2

Fours be with Us

'Old Man' Honda tries the product. (Honda)

Honda's first four-cylinder motorcycle was the RC160, designed to contest the 1959 All Japan Championship (the 'RC' prefix signified works road racer, but confusingly was also applied to motocrossers, and 'CR' could mean the same). Displacing 250cc and featuring twin bevel gear-driven cams and four valves per cylinder, the 160 appeared in Europe the following year. Originally noted for its sound and reliability more than absolute speed, a modified dry-sump version ridden by Bob McIntyre blew the opposition apart in the '61 TT, almost clocking a 100 mph lap. The racing Four was constantly evolving, giving around 40 bhp at 13,000 rpm by this stage with a safe limit of 17,000 rpm.

After an increasingly amazing Grand Prix presence with one-, two-, three-, four-, five- and six-cylinder engines, at the end of the 1967 season Soichiro Honda made the shock announcement that factory racing sponsorship would end. Instead, the effort (and funds) would now be ploughed heavily into the four-wheeled world. The assault on Formula 1 would continue, and there would also be a concerted attack on the everyday transport sector.

Previous attempts to capture part of this potentially lucrative consumer marker had mixed fortunes. Still, history records that Honda's first production four-cylinder engine appeared under the bijou bonnet of the S360 sports car first seen at the 1962 Tokyo Motor Show. Intriguingly, the same motor powered the T360 'mini truck', which was really Honda's first four-wheeler.

RC160. The first Four, in this case equipped with knobbly tyres suitable for Japanese road races of the era. (Honda)

RC148/149: five cylinders, 125cc, 20,000 rpm and eight gears. (Honda)

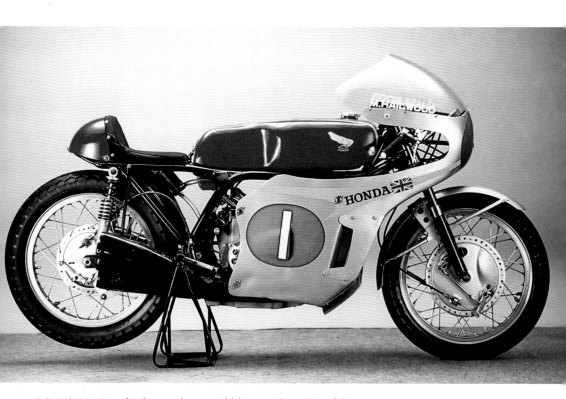

RC165/166: six cylinders and a sound like no other. (Honda)

RC181: 500cc Four with about 80 bhp at 12,000 rpm. (Honda)

Meanwhile, Honda's first road-going Four was installed in the S-series sports cars. This is the ultimate 800cc version. (Rod Ker)

S800 came as a coupe or roadster. (Rod Ker)

Apart from being cooled by water rather than air, the S360 engine and its enlarged variations did share some elements with the RC multis. Twin overhead cams prodded the valves open, and the crankshaft ran in needle-roller bearings. This had the advantage of strength and an ability to cope with a low-pressure lubrication system, but was expensive to make. Like the racers, the little Four effectively had a carburettor for each cylinder by means of two double-choke Keihins. If ever an engine was built to rev, this was it.

Designed to fit in with Japan's 'Kei' class (an economy car of strictly controlled size and power), like the early bikes the S-series was a curious mix of high and low tech. The jewel-like engine contrasted strongly with its primitive separate chassis and crude suspension – the live rear axle was initially driven by a chain, which had been passé in the automotive field since the 1920s. A normal prop shaft came later, and the engine was expanded three times to 531cc, 606cc and finally 791cc for the S800. 70 bhp at 8,000 rpm was the claim, a specific output of 88 bhp/litre. This was astonishing in an era where half that figure was considered reasonable for British rivals like the MG Midget and Triumph Spitfire. 1967 motorists just didn't know what to make of it.

The same sort of culture shock was soon to afflict motorcyclists ...

3

The First Superbike Arrives

CB450 was a slight disappointment, and it was unrealistic to expect it to compete against 650 twins. (Rod Ker)

The CB450 twin had fallen short of expectations – literally, when considering its odd capacity. Strange but true, the British probably thought more of it than the Americans, who were the main customers for 'English' bikes, and firmly believed in the adage, 'there's no substitute for cubes'. In other words, the bigger the better. Whether the 450 matched the speed of an average 'Tribsaton 650' or Harley-Davidson V-twin, it could never have the same relaxed, torquey power characteristics. So why buy one, ran Uncle Sam's logic.

The man in charge of the project, Yoshiro Harada, assessed feedback from US dealers. At about the same time, news leaked out that after an extended gestation BSA/Triumph was going to launch a 750cc Triple. In autumn 1967, the conclusion was that Honda needed to make a four-cylinder bike of equal capacity, but with more sophistication and power than anything else available. According to lore, the 67 bhp target was chosen because it was 1 bhp more than Harley-Davidson could manage with a much larger V-twin engine. Looking back to the late 1960s, it's again ironic that Harley apparently had a 1-litre, four-cylinder prototype on the drawing board, but the management decided there was no market for such a thing!

In 1969 the opposition included the infamous Kawasaki two-stroke triples. (Rod Ker)

Right: Norton's Commando was awarded the *Motorcycle News* Machine of the Year honours for four years.

Below: Triumph Trident T140 and its BSA Rocket III brother beat the CB750 to the market in 1969. (Rod Ker)

Pilot's eye view of the CB750. Huge cow-horn handlebars were normal in the 1960s. (Rod Ker)

Honda's team began work on the project in February 1968, buoyed by the news that the company was now officially the world's largest motorcycle manufacturer. Some engineering targets were laid down:

1. Stability and comfort for high-speed (100 mph) cruising.
2. Brakes that could reliably cope with the weight and speed.
3. Low noise and vibration levels, with an ergonomic riding position, all contributing to reduced rider fatigue.
4. Reliability of ancillary electrics and instruments.
5. Easy maintenance and long service life.
6. Design for latest mass-production techniques.

Meeting their goals involved those relatively new-fangled things called computers to streamline the development process, and utilising expertise gained from GP racing. At least, that was the claim. In practice, the 750 was very different from what had gone before, road or racer, and no doubt required an awful lot of hard graft and inspiration from human engineers with sharp pencils, most of whom had also worked on the GP cars and bikes.

The early prototype apparently had its cylinders and upper crankcase cast in one piece: advanced technology for the time that didn't become a production reality until many years later. Other distinguishing features were four plain black silencers, a front drum brake and a chrome-sided fuel tank which gave the bike an old-fashioned air. Disc brakes had been under consideration from the beginning, but the decision to fit one was only made at the eleventh hour, just before the CB750 was unveiled at the Tokyo show in October 1968.

Honda studio shot of the first CB750. (Honda)

Ostentatious collection of four exhaust pipes, as seen from a journalists' vantage point. (Rod Ker)

The rumour mill had been grinding away by this time. Honda would be launching either a bigger twin based on the DOHC CB450, or a four-cylinder 650 based on two smaller twins stuck together, it was alleged. Power outputs of 80 bhp at 10,000 rpm were mentioned. In fact, the CB750 motor was relatively tame, all-new and shared very little with previous efforts, apart from a chain-driven overhead camshaft. To reduce width, the drive sprocket was in the middle of the crankshaft, alongside the pair of heavy-duty chains responsible for primary drive to the all-indirect gearbox.

Living in horizontally split cases (unlike the rival British Triple, which went to great length to avoid something that was so obviously better, had the casting facilities and machine tools been available), the crankshaft was a major departure from Honda's customary pressed-together affair with rolling element bearings. Instead, the Four used a one-piece forging running split shell main and big end bearings, as seen in 99.9 per cent of cars designed in the second half of the twentieth century. Why? Although plain bearings are less rugged than rollers and will quickly fail if starved of clean oil, they are quieter, cheaper, better suited to volume production and aid cooling. It's also worth noting that Honda had moved to plain bearings on the twelve-cylinder Formula 1 engines.

Four's wet sump engine meant leak-prone external piping and a separate oil tank. (Rod Ker)

The clutch unit was easily accessed through side casing. (Rod Ker)

Interestingly, the CB750 had dry sump lubrication, with a separate 7-pint reservoir of oil in a tank under the seat. Early Honda C71 twins had used a similar system, but later variants were all wet sump, which saves space and is less likely to give rise to problems with oil draining down through the pump when the engine isn't running, resulting in a cloud of smoke and leaks when started. Traditionally, almost all British bikes had a separate supply of oil for the transmission – the belief being that gears needed a different type of lubricant – but the million-selling Mini launched in 1959 had shown that gearboxes were happy enough sharing the same vital fluid.

At the other end of the primary chains, a multi-plate clutch that was easily able to cope with the available power (at least partly because it was turning at close to crankshaft speed so had less torque to transmit) drove what had become a staple feature of Japanese bikes, a five-speed all-indirect gearbox, with drum-type selector forks. More unusually, instead of having the sprocket for the rear drive chain on the end of the layshaft, Honda put it on another gear-driven shaft further back. There are theories as to why this was done.

If only rear chains had been this good in 1969! (Rod Ker)

Firstly, the extra stage meant that the engine didn't have to run backwards in relation to the wheels, which can allegedly affect handling. This idea tends to be disproved by various bikes that do have 'backwards engines' as a consequence of their transmission layout! Alternatively, Honda perhaps found adding an extra shaft enabled the drive sprocket to be closer to the swing arm pivot.

True or not, in practice the extra stage increased mechanical noise and probably made the transmission less smooth, which in real life became some of the less welcome CB750 traits. In particular the bike developed a reputation for breaking rear chains, with serious consequences.

The engine's top half generally followed Honda's established pattern for the single overhead cam small twins (CB125/175/250/350 K-series), except that the camshaft and rockers were carried in two discrete housings bolted to the cylinder head. As a result, the main casting was vastly simpler than the CB450 head, and a little heavier despite two extra cylinders. Nevertheless, the 750's top-end design could, and did, cause owners considerable grief in later years, as shall be discussed later.

Although Honda was the acknowledged master of high-revving four-strokes, to reduce engine width the 750 used an undersquare (bore less than stroke) configuration of 61 × 63 mm, giving a true capacity of 736cc. Generally speaking, undersquare (aka misleadingly 'long stroke') engines are less high-revving than oversquare configurations because piston speeds are greater and there's less room in the combustion chamber for valves. All things being equal, there's also less time for the compressed fuel/air mixture to burn. In practice many more factors have an influence, with the result that some very oversquare engines are known for low-speed torque and some long-stroke engines love to rev!

Breathing through a quartet of Keihin 28 mm slide carburettors operated by separate cables, the Four's maximum power of 67 bhp arrived at 8,000 rpm, while torque peaked at 7,000 rpm and 44 ft/lb. The red line was drawn at a conservative (for Honda) 8,500 rpm. Incidentally, 68 bhp was sometimes quoted as maximum power, sometimes at 8,500 rpm,

Quadruple Keihin carburettors opened by separate cables until 'K0'. (Rod Ker)

but it seems that the inconsistency was due to confusion with the metric PS (Pferde Starke) standard favoured by Honda. 1 PS = 0.9863 bhp, so in practice there's not much difference.

Although the CB750's specification, especially a torque peak just 1,000 rpm lower than maximum power, suggested that it would be a rev-happy screamer like its twin-cylinder ancestors, the reality was that the Four was very mildly tuned and would pull top gear virtually from tick-over to 120 mph. Contrary to expectations, the British Triple opposition had far more frenetic characteristics and needed a lot of revs and gear shifting to produce the same performance. Unfortunately, early Tridents and BSA Rocket IIIs only had four-speed boxes but really needed five, whereas the CB750 could have coped with four quite easily.

Moving to the all-important electrical ancillaries, a large three-phase 210 W alternator went on the left of the crank, with two sets of points to trigger the ignition on the right, all enclosed in smooth aluminium alloy and chrome. The complete engine was said to contribute 80 kg to the bike's not inconsiderable weight. 'Said to' because whatever the workshop manual says, when CB750 engines are actually put on scales they tend to be nearer 100 kg! Precisely what the whole bike weighed is also a moot point because various figures were quoted, the lowest being 445 lb (202 kg), as per contemporary US adverts. Whatever the fisherman's tales, 235 kg seems to be closer to the truth for a bike with all its liquids.

In comparison, British 650cc twins of the era were around 200 kg, while the BSA/ Triumph Triples were first quoted as 210–225 kg, although again even the top estimate

31

Clear instruments, with a quite conservative redline by Honda standards. (Rod Ker)

appears to have been suspect. The last T160 Trident (a fairer yardstick because it had an electric starter and five-speed gearbox) was about 250 kg, again depending on who was doing the weighing.

Still, with due allowance for advertorial optimism, in the sixties and seventies motorcycle designers weren't overly concerned about a few extra pounds here and there. If they had, the CB750 would never have been lumbered with a double-skinned exhaust pipe and individual silencer for each cylinder, but who cared about an extra 5 kg?! What mattered, of course, was broadcasting to the world that you were riding the Honda Four, the first 'superbike'.

In most other respects the CB750 was really quite conventional. Press-button electric starting should have been no big deal in 1969, when we could transplant human hearts and put men on the moon. Yet it was a step ahead of the British, who could design supersonic aircraft and win the Eurovision Song Contest but still struggled on with car and motorcycle industries that were rooted in the 1930s. The Triumph Trident opposition required vigorous kicking for another six years, by which time it was really too late. Flashing indicators were also old hat, but the novelty was that, unlike Lucas, Honda's suppliers made reliable electrics that weren't crippled by vibration and water ingress.

A powerful four-cylinder engine is no use without a suitable chassis. While early Japanese bikes had justifiably been criticised for their rudimentary frames and suspension, a string of Honda GP victories proved that the rest of the world no longer had an edge in this department. So, the CB750 had a wide double-cradle trellis that at least looked strong in all the right places, and was similar in form to that of the RC racers. The only slightly unorthodox component was the swinging arm, which was made up of welded pressings rather than traditional round tubes.

Above: Possibly unnecessary, but essential
for one-upmanship purposes. (Rod Ker)

Right: Square-section Avon SM
rear tyre – probably not the best choice
for a CB750.

The later Roadrunner was much more suitable.

No surprises in the suspension, either, with telescopic forks leading the way and a pair of combined spring/dampers taking care of the swinging arm. Wheel travel was quoted as 5.6 inches (142 mm) front, 3.3 inches (82mm) rear. Early road testers insisted the ride was hard, but times change. As befits a practical, comfortable bike with plush seating for two, the ride was really quite soft and certainly nothing like the teeth-rattling sports motorcycles we've been accustomed to since the 1990s. Unlike the Triumph Trident, which sported a pair of specially designed Dunlop TT100 tyres of 'trigonal' profile and low sidewalls, the Honda made do with a more traditional Dunlop 4.00 × 18 inch rear boot and a 3.25 × 19 inch ribbed front, which probably helped smooth its progress over rough surfaces at the expense of some handling precision.

But what about that shiny 290 mm hydraulic disc attached to the front wheel for braking purposes? Although this was a production motorcycle first, the technology had been around for a couple of decades, initially on planes, then in racing cars, then in road cars. By 1969 even the most humble runabouts had a pair of 'bacon slicers' inside the front arches, so why did it take so long for the concept to be applied to two-wheelers, even for racing?

As ever, one reason was probably expense. Hydraulic systems had to be made to very close tolerances, and paying licence fees to Lockheed or Girling might add to the cost. Also on the negative list, attaching a disc to a wire wheel tended to result in a narrower hub and less spoke triangulation. Not good, but also not really a problem until double discs were introduced in the 1970s, almost obliging the switch to cast alloy wheels, or, in Honda's case, Comstars.

Right: Most bikes are now fitted with modern tyres of slightly wider section than the original 4.00-inch. (Rod Ker)

Below: The 1969 Honda brochure gave plenty of detail.

CB750   DREAM

ENGINE

Type	OHC four cylinder, transverse in-line 4-stroke, aluminium alloy, air cooled
Cylinder capacity	736 cc (44·9 cu in)
Bore × stroke	61 × 63 mm (2·4 × 2·48 in)
Compression ratio	9:1
Carburettors	Four 1·1 in (28 mm) Venturi, piston valve, double float, PW 28
Starting	Electric and kick
Ignition	Coil – battery 12 v 14 ah
Lubrication	Dry sump, separate oil tank
Spark plugs	NGK D-8ES
Clutch	Wet 7 friction disc 5·5 in (140 mm), left hand lever
Transmission	5-speed, constant mesh, left foot pedal return change
Gear ratios	1st 2·500, 2nd 1·708, 3rd 1·333, 4th 1·097, 5th 0·039

PERFORMANCE

Horsepower	67 bhp/8,000 rpm
Torque	6·1 kg/m (44 ft lb)/7,000 rpm
Braking distance	36 ft (11 m) at 31 mph (50km/h)
Turning circle	16 4 ft (5 m)

FRAME

Type		Tubular double cradle
Fuel tank capacity		3 9 gal (4·7 US gal, 18 lit) including reserve
Reserve capacity		1·1 gal (1·3 US gal, 5 lit)
Oil system capacity		6 pts (0·93 US gal, 3·5 lit)
Tyres :	Front	3·25 — 19. Air pressure 28 lb/sq in (2 kg/sq cm)
	Rear	4·00 — 18. Air pressure 30 lb/sq in (2·1 kg/sq cm)
Brakes :	Front	Hydraulic disc, 11·7 in (296 mm), right hand lever

	Rear	7 in (180 mm) full width hub, right foot pedal operation
Suspension :	Front	Hydraulic damped telescopic fork, oil capacity 220/230 cc
	Rear	Swinging arm

DIMENSIONS

Overall length	85 in (2,160 mm)
Overall width	35 in (855 mm)
Overall height	44 in (1,120 mm)
Wheelbase	57·3 in (1,455 mm)
Ground clearance	6·3 in (160 mm)
Seat height	31 in (800 mm)
Footrest height	12 in (310 mm)
Kerb weight (full tank)	481 lb (218 kg)

35

Beyond that, a rotor mounted on a motorcycle tends to get much wetter than one hiding inside a car wheel, which makes a significant difference to performance. In addition, car discs are (or were before the advent of spoked alloys and ultra-low-profile tyres) practically invisible, so they could be made of cast iron which goes red-rusty overnight but retains most of its initial 'bite'. Honda believed that a crusty chunk of iron would look out of place on a gleaming new CB750, so they had to make the disc out of stainless steel, which with the brake pad technology of the 1960s resulted in a drastic reduction in efficiency. Applying the front brake when the rotor was cold and wet could result in a long delay before anything happened. It was something of an embarrassment that an ancient motorcycle fitted with a drum brake operated by a flimsy Bowden cable could actually be safer in everyday use. Doubly so when manufacturers began fitting discs to the rear wheel as well, cleverly eliminating the best chance of stopping in heavy rain.

Honda and the other Japanese manufacturers introducing discs in the 1970s circumvented the issue by assuming that most motorcycles were going to be sold in the US to fair weather riders, not soggy Europe where it rained virtually every day. Astonishingly, it took another fifteen years before motorcycles had dependable brakes in all conditions. In a misguided attempt to address the problem, as late as 1982 Honda introduced the CBX550 Four with enclosed discs, thereby combining the worst features of both types of brake. After years of experimentation with all manner of drilled holes,

Having completed its photographic role, the first production CB750 imported to Britain was loaned to magazines for test reports.

Hitting the open road – sixties style.

Early disc brake calipers were silver. Satin black came later. (Rod Ker)

Stainless steel rotor didn't rust, but caused problems in the wet ... (Rod Ker)

slots and grooves, the eventual solution involved new combinations of rotor and friction material, but that didn't help all those riders who had suffered potentially dangerous wet-weather lag for so long.

Apart from any problems caused by using a stainless disc, Honda's front brake was a curious design, using a single piston caliper mounted on a short swinging arm. Applying the brake resulted in the two pads squeezing the rotor, but the geometry of it meant that the friction surfaces weren't parallel. One of the 'pucks', therefore, had to rock slightly in the caliper, while the other one tended to develop a curved profile. Unfortunately, the rocking pad often seized up in the caliper bore (steel in aluminium equals corrosion), resulting in lots of squeal but not much retardation.

Above: Sometimes a good old-fashioned drum, as fitted to the CB450, was preferable. (Rod Ker)

Right: Honda's efforts to make brakes that worked in all weathers eventually produced inboard discs. (Rod Ker)

4

Into Production

Returning to 1968, the CB750 that debuted at the Tokyo show on 25 October looked very much like the one that became available for public consumption the following year, but it was by no means ready for production. While getting this far in a matter of months was an achievement in itself, there was still plenty of work to do.

In January 1969, 2,000 US Honda dealers were invited to a convention in Las Vegas where the new 750 was the centrepiece. Even if something special had been expected, the Four was a sensation. Not only did it make everything else on the market look quaint, the proposed $1,495 price tag (about $10,000 in 2015 terms), slightly undercutting the BSA and Triumph Triples, was a knockout blow.

As unveiled at the Brighton show the following April, the UK price differential was reversed, but the most blinkered Britophile could see that £650 for an electric start, five-speed, disc-braked OHC Four seemed like better value than £615 for a kick-started, four-speed, drum-braked OVH Triple. Realistically, the Trident's only remaining USP was handling, while the Rocket III looked 'different', and, according to many onlookers, not in a positive way.

Honda had apparently been cautious in predicting demand. Such was the rush of orders that a forecast production of 1,500 per year became a monthly figure. Eventually the target became 35,000 per annum. The snag was that the Saitama factory wasn't capable of making the engine in such numbers. Five a day was a struggle, 100 an impossibility. The car-type crankshaft was a particular problem because existing lines and tooling weren't geared up for the necessary machining operations.

Rave reviews in the press ensured that everyone wanted a 750 Four, but few could actually find one to buy. Inevitably, a black market developed and bikes were said to be changing hands for up to $4,000. Two years passed before production was transferred to a dedicated facility at Suzaka, which had the capacity to meet demand. Who knows how many more units would have been sold if they'd been freely available from the beginning?

It seems that all the early test reports were conducted on what were pre-production models and therefore significantly different in detail from the retail machines that started to appear in American dealers in summer 1969. Umpteen magazines ran features in the first year, not just specialist motorcycle publications, either, such was the level of interest. It's doubtful that Honda needed any more customers, but the front cover photos and ads came thick and fast: 'Sooner or Later, You Knew Honda Would do it'; 'Honda Has More to Move You'; 'The Right Choice' were some of the promises or premises in the US.

'And what about all those nice people?' another copywriter asked, alluding to the company's most famous slogan about Honda clientele. Quite what this meant, if anything, is open to interpretation. Presumably the message was that you could be naughty and nice if you bought a CB750 capable of 125 mph and a standing ¼-mile in 12.6 seconds.

Whatever, this being the age of 'guestimated' gross horsepower, outside an adman's imagination those figures looked very optimistic for a machine with cow horn handlebars and about 300 kg of bike plus rider to shift with 67 bhp: 115 mph and a 13.7s quarter were more likely. Suspicions that the first road-test bikes weren't representative of production models were confirmed by later events: Honda still claimed 67 bhp until 1975, but somehow the top speed was down to about 110 mph and acceleration figures were much slower. To be fair, the same applied to most cars and motorcycles in the 1970s, when manufacturers could no longer get away with quoting fanciful power outputs.

Kawasaki's Z650 ran rings around the 750s. (Rod Ker)

Magnificent, yes, but was the power output 67 bhp or 68 bhp?! (Rod Ker)

Honda's smaller Fours were of nominally 350, 400, 500 and 550cc capacities. Wet-sumped engines were very different from 750.

5

K-Series Variations on a Theme

This is where the story becomes more complicated. As described in the previous chapter, the CB750 was a victim of its own success, causing a huge headache with meeting demand. As a consequence very little happened according to plan, which was a surprise for the world's largest motorcycle manufacturer. So, although at a glance the original 1969 model wasn't vastly different from the ones sitting in your five-star Honda dealer right up to 1975, much had changed under the skin. Many or most components had been altered once the bike was in production.

Even using the term 'production' is tricky because, as we've seen, the first Fours shown were really handmade prototypes. Honda would have had to add a few noughts to the price tag to sell a bike with a crankshaft machined from a steel billet, for instance! All proper production models from engine 1000008-on had forged cranks.

Four bikes went to Las Vegas, where dealers were encouraged to ride flat-out across the desert until they broke down or ran out of gas. Two then went on show in Brighton. One of those promptly disappeared, but the other gold one did the magazine rounds before being sold to the Earl of Denbigh, one of Britain's swinging sixties celebrity toffs, who happened to be a very enthusiastic motorcyclist when he wasn't managing rock bands. Alas, it was later dismantled and seemingly never put back together again. Another of the US quartet apparently ended its days in an American scrapyard sometime in the 1990s. Meanwhile, the Candy-Blue/Green beauty from Vegas resurfaced in the twenty-first century and in 2014 fetched $147,100 at auction.

Pre-production bikes like the quartet of globe-trotting CB750s had four-digit serial numbers. Production models adopted a seven-digit system, CB750-1000001/CB750E-1000001. How many of the lower numbers actually reached retail customers isn't clear. In any case, note that Honda engine and frame numbers don't match.

The first 7414 bikes in the series were the so-called 'sand-cast' models, which feature distinctively rough engine crankcases. While everyone accepts the term and how these relative rarities can be identified, it's generally acknowledged now that the cases technically weren't sand-cast and were actually made by a gravity-casting process that gives a less smooth finish than the high-pressure die-casting normally employed by Big H.

It's interesting that even Honda Heritage's own CB750 development history refers to 'sand-molded crankcases'. Sand may be involved, but it isn't sand-casting!

Some sources suggest that early bikes were hand-built at Honda's California base until September 1969, after which mass production began in Japan. There seems to be no supporting evidence for that from those who worked there.

Apart from the crankcases, the first model's main identification points are cable-operated carburettors, large louvred side panels carrying five-sided badges, a humped rear seat and plastic instrument lenses. The sand-cast survival rate is poor, in part due to the Four's unfortunate habit of throwing its drive chain, which could cause enough damage to write off the crankcases. A proper repair would, of course, involve a new engine or a replacement set of superior die-cast cases. Failure of the output shaft bearings had the same disastrous effect and was by no means uncommon. All of which means that genuinely original 1969 CB750s are rare and expensive, although rest assured that $147,100 is not typical.

Apart from 'Rollo' Denbigh's personal wheels, no CB750s were registered in the UK before 1970, when a trickle of production was finally diverted from the all-important US market. Rarest of all, a mere thirty-six of the retrospectively named K0, distinguished by its bell-crank throttle linkage, were sold in Britain.

Odd though it may seem now, for many years Honda SOHC Fours were not considered worthy of much attention, so a lot of these early bikes were shunted off to breakers, or what we now see as butchered for customisation. Interest picked up in the late 1990s and 2000s, which resulted in considerable numbers of 1970s Japanese bikes, including CB750s, Suzuki GT750s and Kawasaki Z1s, finding their way across the Atlantic. As a result, some models in standard trim are probably easier to find in Britain now than they were thirty or forty years ago. The bad news is that prices have escalated because they're still rare!

It's curious that after the initial surge of enthusiasm and concomitant superlative overload in the press, attitudes to the CB750 changed rapidly as we headed into the 1970s. Perhaps because Brits couldn't forgive Honda for out-supering the BSA-Triumph Triples, test reports tended to be increasingly negative: 'You could have bought a car for that much' was a common insult.

Typifying the insular mood, the universe's top-selling and influential weekly paper, *MotorCycle News,* voted the Norton Commando Machine of the Year from 1968 until 1972, when the 903cc DOHC Kawasaki Z1 finally usurped it. For those who don't know, the Commando was a 750/850 twin based on a thirty-year-old engine stretched to the limit. Although it did go very well on the sadly rare occasions when it was going, and had a novel means of vibration control, in so many ways it was a warranty claim on wheels. Soichiro Honda must have been bemused that his fast and reliable 750 Four should be snubbed in favour of a machine that often needed a complete rebuild after a few thousand miles. Patriotism was a force to be reckoned with half a century ago!

In June 1971, the updated CB750K1 appeared in the UK. Essentially the same as the original, alterations to the seat, side panels and oil tank subtly modernised the styling – not to everyone's taste, it must be added. On a practical level, changes to the fuel tank were claimed to increase capacity, but in practice this doesn't seem to be true! In fact, it appears that the main change occurred after about 400 bikes had been built, when the tank underside was modified to add more clearance for the carburettor cables. This actually

One of Norton's famously gratuitous adverts for the Commando.

Workshop manuals for British bikes tended to be battered through use, while Honda ones typically only had a few oily fingerprints in the chain adjustment section! (Rod Ker)

BSA's 1971 range was spearheaded by the Rocket III. Production only lasted another year.

reduced capacity by a couple of litres. Due to a combination of power, contemporary metallurgy and a harsh transmission, the '750 Four', as it said on the new side panels, suffered greatly from drive chain wear. In an effort to tame its appetite, an adjustable oil feed was fitted to the gearbox output shaft.

Criticism of the handling was addressed by a slightly harder set of rear springs, which can't have impressed all those who claimed the suspension was already too harsh. Although Hondas officially never leak oil, modifications to the forks, with larger outside diameter seals, made the unthinkable less of a possibility.

Barely six months later the K2 arrived, again with only minor (visible) changes, but with a new serial number series starting at CB750E 2000001. Painted fork shrouds and headlamp brackets had given way to chrome plate, while a new central pod of warning lights had sprouted from the handlebar clamps between the two main instruments. The dreaded turn-signal beeper 'safety feature' was introduced on the K2, but it didn't take very long to discover that an infuriating beep was more confusing than helpful to other road users. Most British riders disconnected the device ASAP.

Also on the agenda, a lockable seat with a helmet-securing hook and compartment to keep the owners' manual appeared, along with alterations to the rear brake lever and sprocket retaining bolts. If you did have the misfortune to break down or run out of petrol, at least you could amuse yourself by reading the unintentionally hilarious 'Japanglish' booklet!

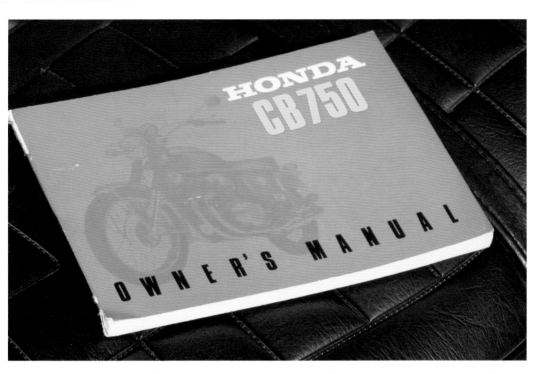

Honda owners' manuals tended to be pristine, only partly because they contained hardly any useful information. (Rod Ker)

With Honda seemingly concentrating all its efforts on developing cars like the Civic and its clever CVCC (Compound Vortex Controlled Combustion) stratified charge engine, which met forthcoming emissions standards without using a catalytic converter, the motorcycle side stagnated. The K2 was the current model in Britain until the end of 1975, firmly relegated to also-ran status by Kawasaki's 'King Z'. This was some sort of poetic justice because Kawasaki had been developing a 750cc Four of their own when Honda beat it to the market in 1969, forcing a complete redesign. Whether Honda's rush to get the CB750 into production was prompted by whispers about Kawasaki's plans we shall never know, but after the Z1 hit the streets Honda was fighting a losing battle. Given a straight choice few UK customers would have considered yesterday's Honda, which was inferior in nearly every department. Most of all, with a 167cc deficit the CB was comprehensively vanquished by the 82 bhp Kaw, which had a 15 mph speed edge and would cover a standing ¼-mile at least a second quicker.

However, by this time, a lot of Americans, particularly the touring crowd, had grown attached to their (mostly) faithful Cee-Bees, so the US progressed through K3, K4 and K5 variants. K3s had another rear suspension update, now with five-way adjustable spring preload. There were also new forks, with stanchions telescoping directly through the sliders instead of in replaceable bushes. Altered piston rings reduced oil consumption. That was about it except for a revised wiring and fuse system. The front brake grew a small shroud – it was never clear whether this was intended to keep water off the disc or the rider!

Launched in 1972, the Kawasaki Z1 made the Honda Four look almost obsolete. (Rod Ker)

Double overhead camshafts and another 15 bhp left Honda standing. (Rod Ker)

Moving on, only a very dedicated Honda spotter would appreciate that the K4 had slightly different petrol tank stripes. The K5 was more easily rumbled as it had a fuel tap moved from the right to the left side, which was far more sensible as you could keep the throttle open when the tank ran onto reserve. Pre-K5 this was less of a problem because the twist grip was friction-adjustable, but that useful facility was now history, much to the disgruntlement of the long-distance crew. It seems that this was another safety feature, inspired by US blame culture.

Nevertheless, some of the measures introduced to protect ourselves from ourselves really did work. For example, the K5 also introduced a hinged piece of rubber attached to the end of the side stand in such a way that it would be flipped up by the first left-hand bend if the rider forgot. Very few motorcyclists hadn't forgotten at least once, so here was a simple yet effective way of preventing accidents.

Honda enthusiast and Four expert Chris Rushton has owned about twenty-five CB750s, including this much-travelled sand-cast model, seen here in the Isle of Man, Scotland and the Lake District. It's a 1969 model that was first registered in the USA and has now clocked a trouble-free 130,000 miles, remarkably still with original exhausts. (Chris Rushton)

Above: Five-sided badge of pre-K1 models. (Rod Ker)

Left: First model available in either Candy Ruby-Red or Candy Blue-Green. Original paintwork and graphics that are hard to reproduce. (Rod Ker)

A K1 in Candy Gold. Note smaller side panels and painted headlamp brackets. (Chris Rushton)

Not much space left for a battery and toolkit. (Rod Ker)

6

Branching out with the F-Series

1975 and 1976 were radical years by recent Honda standards. Introduced in October 1975, the CB750F Super Sports, as it said on the fuel tank, really did look different ... different, but any beauty seemed to be restricted to the eyes of the designer. The average motorcyclist perceived the F and its almost identical twin, the F1, as an awkward mash of ideas. Never mind that lemon paintwork, the 4-1 exhaust and seat looked as if they were designed to fit another bike. Nothing gelled.

That may have been acceptable if the F1 (the initial plain F was only sold on the US market) had been superior in any major respect. But it really wasn't, and the Super Sports tag seemed to have little foundation. Although press reports were quite positive, the general feeling was that journalists might have been less impressed if they had been splashing around Chiswick in the rain rather than riding through sun-kissed Spain. Of direct relevance, one of the 'improved' features was a rear disc brake, which could be as treacherous as the one at the front in wet weather. Fashion seemed to be the only justification, because due to what is commonly referred to as 'weight transfer' the rear wheel of a motorcycle can only supply a small percentage of braking. It was therefore doubly dubious to fit a twin-piston caliper to the back, which potentially could provide more power than the much-criticised swinging setup at the other end.

Apart from the obvious cosmetics, there was much confusion about exactly what had been altered in the engine and chassis. Even Honda didn't seem sure, but the theory was that the frame had extra strength and increased wall thickness. Perhaps. Of more certainty, the steering geometry gave less trail, while the wheelbase was ½ inch longer. While Big H was coy about disclosing a power output, early estimates were that about 10 bhp had been added thanks to a higher compression ratio, a fiercer camshaft profile and altered valve angles.

In practice the extra horsepower was illusory, so performance was almost identical to the contemporary K-series – which translated as 'fairly slow' in the rapidly evolving three-quarter-litre class. In fact, the new Honda CB550F was almost as fast (or slow), and cost about 20 per cent less, which must have been a corporate embarrassment. However, beyond numbers on a piece of paper, the problem was that the F1 just didn't have the zing of more modern designs. Yamaha and Suzuki had brand new 750s (GS750 and XS750) looming on the horizon, and Kawasaki was about to launch a Z650 that was faster and cheaper than the lot.

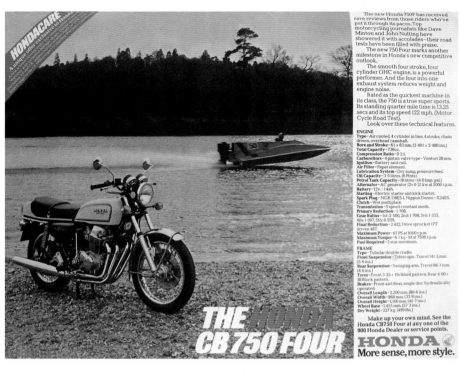

CB750F arrived in 1975, ostensibly to replace four pipers.

CB550F was almost as fast but much cheaper.

Modest claims for the heavily revised F2.

Handling? Better, but nothing special. Again, the new upstarts had the edge. Same for brakes, gearboxes, mechanical quietness, switches, instruments, lights, etc. There were whispers that the build quality was worse, too. How could Honda, the superbike's creator, get it so wrong? The intention had been for the F1 to supersede the K2 in Britain, but, faced with a four-pipe customer mutiny, in mid-1976 it was decided to bring back the original in the latest K6 guise. This borrowed a few F components, such as the swinging arm and an output shaft with no chain oiler, but effectively we were back in 1972.

There followed about a year during which Britain's motorcyclists were not flocking to their local Honda dealers to buy CB750s (or the genuinely innovative GL1000 Gold Wing, for that matter, a bike which unfairly suffered the brunt of all the 'two-wheeled car' gibes). With tourers' dreams now catered for, rumours were rife that the sleeping giant was about to wake up and launch a much more sporty in-line Four, based on the twin cam derivatives that had been running in endurance racing.

In this instance the rumours were correct, if slightly premature. So it was that in mid-1977 the CB750F2 and CB750K7 appeared in UK showrooms. The four-pipe K had inherited the F2's suspension and F1's engine, complete with F2-type accelerator pump carburettors, which helped deal with increasingly severe American EPA (Environmental Protection Agency) emissions regulations. A fatter, 4.5-inch rear tyre on a smaller 17-inch rim addressed tourers' needs for increased load capacity. In styling terms, the look was now restrained and 'classic', for want of a better word, with a new set of seamless megaphone-type silencers. These were whisper-quiet compared to the rorty 1969 originals, which had been modified internally over the years while keeping the same exterior.

RCB endurance racers were highly successful but differed greatly from road bikes.

Ad copywriter reasoning for buying a Honda!

Away from the tracks, Honda served up a quartet of sensible tourers. The CB750K7 was reintroduced when customers decided they didn't like the F1 or F2.

Honda's commitment to aftersales service was always impressive.

The expenditure continued long after you bought the bike. Few road riders had full leathers in those days, but Honda anticipated the trend.

Clothes, fairings, racks and luggage were all part of the package.

The F2 arrived in time for the 1977 TT races at the Isle of Man, where they were used as marshals' bikes. More publicity was garnered by race ace Phil Read riding a similar bike to victory in the new Formula 1 World Championship series. 'If it works on the track ... Honda put it on the road', trumpeted magazine advertisements. Reading on, Honda had an attack of humbleness and said, 'Probably the fastest and certainly one of the best handling production 750s in the world today ... After starting the 'superbike era' it was inevitable that our competitors followed Honda's lead. It is time once more to take a step ahead.'

That's about the nearest you could get to an admission that the Four had been an also-ran for some years! It would be uncharitable to point out that the string of wins at European endurance events the previous year were on factory-prepared twin cam bikes, which displaced close to a litre and gave rather more power than the 810cc version of the single cam Four, as thrashed round the Isle of Man by Mr Read.

The bike sitting in your friendly neighbourhood Honda showroom wearing a £1,234 price ticket still had a capacity of 736cc, but had benefited from extensive modifications, which merited a new set of serial numbers starting with CB750GE 1000016. The cylinder head was new, with bigger tracts and valves. Inlets were up from 32 mm to 34 mm, exhausts from 28 mm to 31 mm. Although the compression ratio was actually down from 9.2:1 to 9.0:1, the valves were opened by a higher lift camshaft, all resulting in a claimed 73 bhp at 9,000 rpm and a torque curve peaking at 7,500 rpm. To handle the extra strain, the engine's lower end was strengthened. In short, this was a far more sporty effort, even if cynics quipped that it had taken eight years to make a 750 that was as fast as the 1969 model.

On the chassis side, the forks were new and sported a pair of entirely different brake calipers, mounted behind the sliders to reflect the latest thinking about steering and stability. The wheelbase had also grown a bit more to nearly 59 inches, while the suspension was generally harder in springing and damping. As happened elsewhere in the range from 1976, Honda equipped the new F2 with a pair of its innovative Comstar wheels, inherited from the RCB endurance racer.

Made up of pressed steel spokes riveted to an aluminium rim, the idea was to combine the best of traditional wire wheels and the cast alloy ones being introduced by other manufacturers. The result was of mixed success. On appearance alone they had about a 50/50 approval rating, but there were concerns about longevity. Some claimed that Comstars bent very easily in minor prangs and were then scrap. Unlike spoked wheels, which could be tweaked back into line, a wobbly rim could not be trued. Although enterprising mechanics did manage to press Comstars into shape, it wasn't officially condoned.

Other prophets of doom worried about 'electrolytic' corrosion and weakening due to dissimilar metals being riveted together. With the benefit of hindsight, we can see that most of the fears were unfounded. Close to forty years later, some Comstars still look new and run true, while they're quite often attached to swinging arms that have rotted to pieces!

It's worth noting that Honda had good reason to try to reinvent the wheel. As mentioned, disc brakes on spoked hubs, especially in pairs, tended to result in a less triangulated spoke pattern, part of the justification for the move to cast allow wheels.

That dealt with the strength issue, but in most cases only at the cost of extra weight, all the worse because it was unsprung mass and therefore affected the suspension and handling.

Another disadvantage was that one-piece alloys were too rigid, which spoiled the ride and put more stress on the bearings. Running on spoked wheels, a vehicle is effectively hanging on springs, so Comstars were deliberately designed to have 'give'. Some alloys were better than others, of course. BMW and Ducati had problems with cracking, while Yamaha's were over-engineered and weighed what felt like a ton. Interestingly, the RD400 was first available with spoked wheels, a pair of alloys being a £50 option that made it a worse bike. Fashion dictated that everyone was prepared to pay extra to suffer!

While the basics were unchanged and the tank and seat came directly from the F1, the F2 looked much more modern and purposeful, thanks to the wheels, mostly black engine, big alloy footrest hangers and less awkward exhaust terminating in a long silencer. Phil Read took one for a ride round his neighbourhood and in *Motor Cycle* declared it to be 'the most fabulous road bike I've ridden in yonks.' As he was working for Honda, his opinion was perhaps slightly biased, but the F2 generally received a warm reception from magazine testers.

Still, the extra power seemed to be hard to find, residing as it was at 7,000 rpm-plus. Typically for a tuned engine with bigger valves there was less power at lower revs, so riders who couldn't be bother to change gear constantly were disappointed. The lack of

Nostalgia. Strange that it may seem, in the latter 1970s the Triumph Bonneville outsold all other 750s in the UK.

Long before fairings became almost universal on sports bikes, F2-based Phil Read Replica and Honda Britain sported this twin headlamp beauty. (Rod Ker)

No one has ever matched their raw power, classic lines and incredible handling. And probably no one ever will.

The motorcycles that started it all. The bikes from Britain.
Now for 1976, the styling, the power, the handling are here, more together than ever in these latest superbikes from Britain.
The new 1976 Triumph Bonneville T140V, the legendary 750cc vertical twin. The unsurpassed Triumph Trident T160. And the incomparable Norton 850 Commandos with vibration-free Isolastic ride.
It's time to get it on with British Biking. See the full line, now on display at your Norton and Triumph dealers.

Norton Triumph Corporation/Norton Triumph Bonneville Ltd.
2765 East Huntington Drive, Duarte, California 91010.
Phone (213) 359-3221.
CIRCLE NO. 27 ON READER SERVICE PAGE.

No more BSAs, but new T160 Trident and its British buddies were still selling well in 1976.

Both T160 and Mk3 version of Norton Commando featured electric starters. Six years too late for some.

Hondastyle Racing circa 1975. For those not too worried about tyre wear or wardrobe malfunctions.

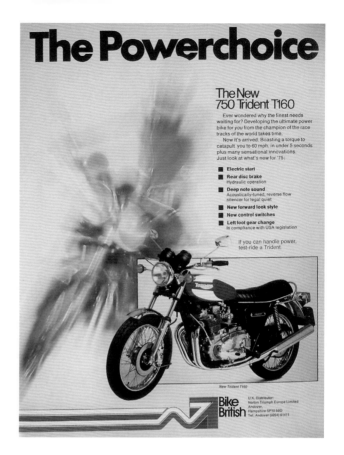

If the T150 Trident had looked as good as the T160, Honda would have sold far fewer CB750s.

torque was also reflected in performance figures: a top speed of around 125 mph was good, but reported standing ¼-mile times were often slower than the F1's, which was easier to launch.

The F2 was the last SOHC CB750 model in Britain and was on sale here until 1979, when the all-new twin cam 750 and 900 arrived. America briefly received a F3 update, but this was scarcely different.

That wasn't quite the end of the story: to capitalise on Read's 1977 TT win, Honda produced a batch of Phil Read Replicas in conjunction with chassis wizard Colin Seeley. Although under the fibreglass skin was basically another CB750F2, there had been many changes – no less than 220 alterations, according to the people who built it. Most obviously, the naked look had gone in favour of a large fairing complete with twin headlights. The side panels stayed, but there was a new seat with room for about one and a half consenting adults, 5 g alloy tank and plastic front mudguard – all colour-matched in Team Honda Britain red, white and blue. The F2's giant silencing apparatus had been supplanted by an equally enormous 'works' black silencer climbing up the right-hand side.

Other goodies included ace handlebars, rear-set brake and gear levers, Girling gas dampers and a relocated ignition switch living inside the fairing rather than in the expected place between the speedometer and rev counter. Many moons later, an ignition switch in the normal site is therefore a way of spotting a Phil Read Replica that wasn't built by Seeley.

Tuned engines with Piper cam and electronic ignition were available, but even with everything left standard the Read Replica certainly looked and sounded the business and had a slight speed edge over a normal F2, thanks to reduced weight and better aerodynamics. Still, there was a price to pay, in all senses. The PRR cost £1,895 – about £350 more than the list of the ordinary model, which in reality was discounted to around £1,350.

Seeley had initially been commissioned to build a hundred bikes. That figure was eventually extended to around 400, but only 150 of those had been completed when there was a disagreement between Honda and Read. The upshot was that the rest of the line had a new name, Honda Britain (or plain CB750SS), and new colours: white/blue, or white/red. Some of these were subsequently returned to the original patriotic livery. It was possible to create a DIY replica version by buying the main parts, so after all these years it may be difficult to establish a bike's true provenance. First appearing in 1978 in time for the TT (where Phil Read failed to repeat his 1977 win), some examples weren't registered until the 1980s and it has been suggested that Honda Britain's real purpose was to shift unsold stocks of F2s.

Comstar wheels, black engine and three disc brakes for the F2. (Chris Rushton)

Above: Long-time go-faster firm, Read Titan, add a new dimension to the F2.

Right: Yamaha offered something completely different in the form of their XS750 Triple with shaft drive and soft suspension.

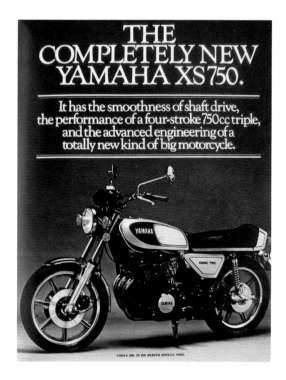

The Phil Read Replica and the re-christened Honda Britain both sported big mean 4-1 exhausts, not quite standard in this case. (Rod Ker)

7

The CB750 Automatic

Honda's original superbike spawned one more unexpected offshoot: the CB750A, which came to market in 1976 after a slightly delayed development period. 'A' stood for 'Automatic', the intention being to create an easy-to-ride machine for all those lazy people who couldn't, or wouldn't, change gear. Technically it wasn't really an automatic because it had two widely spaced gears selected manually, coupled to a torque converter that effectively filled in the gaps. In essence, this all went back to the wildly successful 50cc Honda Cub which was introduced in 1958 and designed so that anyone could ride it, even one-handed if necessary.

Launched slightly earlier, Moto Guzzi's V1000 Convert dabbled with a similar concept, but the 750A was a more sophisticated machine involving almost a completely new engine. Starting with redesigned crankcases, the primary drive was now through a Hy-Vo chain instead of a pair of single-row roller chains. The torque converter was gear driven, taking power to a two-speed gearbox. The novelty here was that these were selected by hydraulic means through multi-plate clutches and not through mechanical forks, as is usual. In some ways, the transmission was a distant ancestor of the multi-speed, double-clutch boxes seen in cars thirty years later.

The A's hydraulics were powered by a separate oil pump, and the lubrication system was now wet sump. Any concerns about using ordinary multi-grade oil instead of ATF (Automatic Transmission Fluid) seemed to be misplaced, or at least not something to worry about for a long time.

The engine itself was comprehensively detuned. Fed by four smaller carburettors of 24 mm with a compression ratio lowered to 8.6:1 and a milder camshaft, maximum power was 47 bhp. This translated into a top speed of 105–110 mph and unimpressive acceleration by motorcycle standards. A standing quarter in around 15.8s was in 250cc territory. As with all autos, or semi-autos, though, the practical performance available was better than the paper figures suggest because riding flat-out was simply a matter of selecting either gear and twisting the throttle wide open.

Some of the technology came straight from the N600 and Civic Hondamatic cars, which the company had been working on since the 1960s. Sharing costs should have saved some money, but the development budget for the 750A must still have been huge. It would all have been worthwhile if clutchless two-wheeled travel had been a hit, but sales were modest

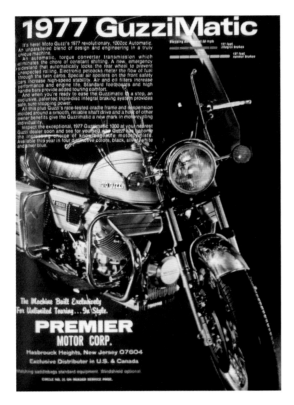

Guzzi came up with a semi-automatic
version of the big V-twin. GuzziMatic in
the US, V1000 Convert in the UK.

Honda spent much time and effort
on the 750A, but most motorcyclists
preferred to change gear.

Introducing the revolutionary new Honda 750 Automatic.

Nothing but nothing can be compared with riding the new Honda 750 Automatic. You're aboard a complex, finely balanced mechanism; every movement you make is returned in kind, without hesitation, with precision that's almost eerie. This is something that's never happened to you before.

The Honda CB-750A is more than just a new touring bike. It's a whole new concept in the sport, bringing unprecedented ease and control to the world of motorcycling because it takes the work out of stop-and-go riding. It simply shifts for itself.

The new Hondamatic transmission does the work for you. It's engineered with two ranges, "low" and "drive," coupled to a smooth hydraulic torque converter. For city riding, use "low" which has a range of from zero to 60. For effortless road cruising, a flick of your left foot selects "drive." That's all there is to it; enjoy the scenery.

But the ingenuity doesn't stop there. When parking the bike, be sure to apply the special parking brake. Just pull the brake cable knob and depress the right pedal. In addition, there's a transmission lock-out feature. When the sidestand is down, the transmission cannot be shifted out of neutral.

Instrumentation is specially designed for this new kind of riding.

The "low" and "drive" ranges are clearly indicated on the large speedometer gauge on the left. All three transmission positions are illuminated on the right-hand gauge. Oil pressure, high

Instrumentation is designed for a new kind of riding. Lights instantly monitor gear selection.

Parking brake. Because the CB-750A transmission automatically moves into "neutral" when the kick stand is down, this feature secures the machine when parked. A Honda exclusive.

Large contoured seat is deeply padded for long-distance touring comfort. Note low-profile rear grab bar. And wide chromed fender to reduce road spray.

beam and turn indicators complete the new warning light system.

Perhaps most important of all, the new 750 Automatic is a Honda. Developed to do *everything* well. From suspension to braking, from comfort to finish and detailing, Honda makes the world's best-selling road bikes, far and away. The new CB-750A is heir to that enviable heritage. It's the news of the year. Automatically.

HONDA
First. For good reason.

CIRCLE NO. 50 ON READER SERVICE PAGE.

Nothing but nothing can be compared with riding the new Automatic, suggested Honda.

and the model only lasted for two years. So far as the UK was concerned, the A didn't exist. A bike was shipped to Britain at TT time for appraisal by the press, in most cases getting a 'What's the point?' verdict. Rather than risk failure it was decided not to import the model. That was probably wise, because the CB400 twin Hondamatic was brought into the UK the following year and didn't sell like hotcakes.

Perhaps surprisingly, Honda gave the 750 Automatic a significant makeover before it was terminated, adding the latest forks and a more elegant exhaust system. The first model had used GL1000 GoldWing spoked wheels with alloy rims, but, in common with the rest of the street bike range, these were supplanted by Comstars.

The change to wet sump had the side effect of freeing up space underneath the seat where the oil tank used to live, allowing the use of a larger battery charged by a higher output 290 W alternator. Firing up a CB750 in cold weather had always been tricky (and autos generally can't be push-started), so here was the almost accidental cure.

Like the Moto Guzzi Convert, the Auto must go down in history as a heroic failure. While riding it without shifting gear was possible, potential buyers were put off by what seemed like more, rather than less, complication. Would it have found a market if it had been a fully automatic 'twist and go' super scooter of the sort that has grown in popularity in Europe over the last two decades? Some sort of fairing and enclosure would undoubtedly have helped, but even the new flagship GL1000 GoldWing was launched as a naked bike with absolutely no weather protection or luggage capacity. It took several years before Honda realised that the vast majority of customers immediately festooned their bikes with extras.

It had an ordinary five-speed gearbox, but the GL1000 GoldWing turned out to be a bike that a lot of people wanted instead of a UJM. (Honda)

8

Go Faster or Slower

The CB750 was fast, of that there was no argument, but, motorcyclists being motorcyclists, as soon as it appeared there was a rush to make it go even faster. A deluge of engine tuners and chassis specialists descended, all claiming to transform the Four.

One who certainly did was Russ Collins, whose CB750-based drag bikes became famous in the 1970s. Collins was working in a Californian bike shop in 1969 when the new Honda arrival spurred him on to start his own business. At the time, Harley-based drag bikes were still pre-eminent, but Russ came up with a 400 bhp supercharged CB750 which ruffled a few feathers.

He then moved up to the Top Fuel class, running a triple-engined beast that in 1973 became the first 7-second ¼-mile bike. Three years later, a serious accident and a long spell in hospital prompted a rethink. Collins campaigned against the very sort of multi-engined machine he was famed for ... but it didn't work! Instead, he created a 2-litre, dual CB750 monster that clocked a 7.3-second run with a terminal speed of close to 200 mph – a record that stood for eleven years.

Apart from his brains and bravery, Russ was a great showman and publicist, and R. C. Engineering became one of the companies synonymous with fast Hondas in the 1970s. When straight Fours were displaced by V4s in the 1980s, RC catered for the new wave, while also moving into specialised fuel-injection systems.

Chiefly in America, other names associated with go-faster CB750s were the legendary Hideo Yoshimura, Powroll Performance and Action 4's. 'Pops' Yoshimura was a self-taught maestro of tuning, who could seemingly improve any engine by altering the cam profile, carburettors and exhaust. Although the Kawasaki Z1 and then the Suzuki GS750 diverted his attention away from the Honda Four in racing, there were still plenty of CB750s on the street benefiting from Yoshimura goodies.

Early Honda Fours were a rarity in the UK, so it took a few years before the tuning cottage industry started to abandon home-grown bikes and turn attention to Japanese Fours. [David] Dixon Racing became the sole European agent for Yoshimura, while Dresda Autos, Read Titan, Rickman and Paul Dunstall were also doing brisk business by the mid-1970s. In most cases, the first step to increased performance involved boring out the liners to increase the capacity to around 810cc, then fitting a sports exhaust and

Back at Read Titan, the sky was the limit for modified single-cam Hondas.

altering the carburettors to suit. Having added power, the rest of the chassis would need uprating, either by modifying the stock components or throwing the frame away and using something better, which Dave Degans at Dresda did with notable success.

This was essentially Honda's brief for the 'CB750' (RC750) which scored a famous victory at the 1970 Daytona 200, humiliating both the British and the Americans in the process. Although officially retired from racing since 1967, in 1970 the quaint AMA regulations designed to give Harley-Davidson V-twins a chance of winning were finally relaxed to make all 750cc bikes eligible. Honda management realised that if they didn't enter a CB750 then someone else would, possibly resulting in a less-than-impressive result. Four very special RC750s were duly put together in Japan, to be ridden by Tommy Robb, Ralph Bryans, Bill Smith (TT specialist and long-time Chester-based Honda dealer) and the previous year's runner up, Dick Mann.

'Rules were made to be broken' was apparently accepted behaviour at Daytona. First it was discovered that the Triumph and BSA Triples were using non-homologated five-speed gearboxes. Honda threatened an official protest, but when Bryans later lost control, fell off and went sliding down the main straight, his bike caught fire. Although that was common enough, the sight of the crankcases going up in flames made it obvious that they were made out of non-standard and expensive magnesium alloy, which was hardly cricket, although not necessarily a huge advantage (the XL250 trailbike of 1972 did, in fact, have magnesium alloy casings). Still, in the circumstances Honda decided not to protest too much about the illicit British gearboxes!

Norton-Triumph liked to remind Honda that they still won a lots of races.

Despite problems with cam chain tensioners and misfires, Mann's bike went the distance and crossed the line a couple of seconds ahead of Gene Romero's Triumph Triple. The other Hondas had retired hurt, and Mann's Four was probably close to expiry, only running on three cylinders and almost out of oil.

Even without the flaming crankcases incident it would be naïve to believe that the RC750 shared much with the CB750 you could buy (if you could find one!) for about $1,500, or £650, but this slimmest of victories must have given plenty of people another excuse not to buy a Harley or a British Triple. In the US the Honda was outselling the Trident and Rocket III by four-to-one. Still, it's worth remembering that against all the odds the British Triples did manage to beat Honda and the rest on many succeeding occasions.

Motorcycle Mechanics gets a chance to try the Rickman CR750.

The F2 was nearing the end when Read Titan gave us the Pursuit MkII, with 2-1 exhaust.

9
Reborn as a Classic

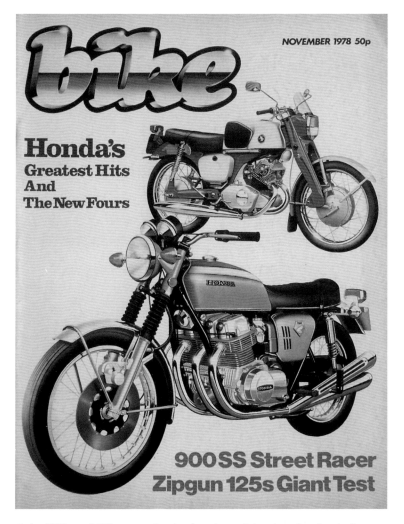

Only 1978, and *Bike* magazine is already anticipating the classic future.

Motorcycle Mechanics offers 750 Four buying advice. Not very relevant in the twenty-first century.

Quoted figures vary wildly, but over half a million CB750 derivatives were made during a production life of almost a decade. Against a generally booming bike market, overall sales fell over the years, culminating in record UK registrations in 1979. As we've seen, once the Kawasaki Z1 appeared the CB750 was considered an also-ran, and the Suzuki GS750 and Kawasaki Z650 added more nails to the coffin. Towards the end of that period Honda's endurance racing exploits generated publicity, but in reality the RCB bikes were far removed from the standard CB750 and effectively acted as prototypes of the succeeding 750/900/1,100cc twin cam, 4-valve per cylinder Fours. The later CBX Six was based on similar parts and could almost be considered a modular version of the same engine. In turn, much of that technology became obsolete after 1982 when Honda decided that water-cooled V4s were the future.

All of which left the original four-cylinder superbike very much out of the limelight until the late 1980s. CB750s were often treated as throwaway items destined to end their days piled unceremoniously in American scrapyards, the survivors waiting for the day when Japanese bikes were recognised as part of our motorcycling heritage. The inevitable eventually happened, and by the 1990s Honda's archetypal UJM (Universal Japanese Motorcycle) was becoming rare enough to earn a classic tag. As per usual, the early 'sand-cast' bikes were the first to be appreciated, but some thirty-five years after the last K8 and F3 rolled out of the factory, all SOHC variants have some classic cachet. Even the F1 and Automatic have admirers!

One of the staple page-fillers in contemporary motorcycle magazines was the *Buyers' Guide*, which gave sage advice about common faults and foibles. In the classic afterlife, much of that once-wise information is irrelevant. For instance, an everyday rider of the 1970s might have been worried by petty things like short-life fork seals and a tendency for the oil filter bolt and tappet covers to round off. Fast forward to the twenty-first century and most old bikes cover only a few hundred miles a year, so fork seals are unlikely to be an issue. Similarly, while all Honda SOHC Fours were deservedly infamous for chewed-up oil filter bolts and sticking tappet covers, in the overall scheme of things these are now inconsequential trifles.

In reality, the chief issues for present day CB750 fanciers centre round non-availability of some new spares and the quest for originality. Once upon a time, Honda was justifiably proud to say that any part for any bike could be supplied, even if it meant setting someone to make it from scratch in a far-flung factory. It would have been unrealistic to expect that policy to continue indefinitely. All restorers are now up against the same problem of unavailability, which can leave you waiting for months to find a few elusive parts to finish an otherwise functional machine.

Following the usual supply-and-demand equation, if enough people are looking for the same part, there will come a time that a third party will step forward and make a batch of pattern replacements. In some cases these will be hugely expensive, and also may or may not be of equal quality to the original. Beggars generally can't be choosers.

One perennial headache for owners concerns the 4-4 exhaust. Water would collect in the lower sections, rust would set in, and within a couple of years holes would appear. There was really no way of preventing this, because exhausts collect condensation even in a dry climate like California. Genuine pipes and silencers were always very expensive, so most bikes were treated to an aftermarket 4-2 or 4-1. This did at least save weight, but many of the claims about boosted power were specious. There was a widespread fallacy that someone welding pipes together in a shed could improve on the efforts of a billion-pound

Specialists like David Silver can now supply most parts, including complete exhaust systems. (Rod Ker)

This slightly seedy 750 shows signs of oil leakage around the head gasket area, a common problem with more than one cause. (Rod Ker)

This is what most exhausts looked like after a couple of years. (Rod Ker)

Any forty-year-old electric system can be forgiven for not looking like new, but it probably still works. (Rod Ker)

Fuel tap on left side means K5 or later. (Rod Ker)

manufacturer's R&D department. In practice, what you could almost guarantee was extra noise and upset carburation, possibly with restricted access to the oil filter and drain plug as a bonus. Also, unlike OE Honda systems, aftermarket replacements had single-skinned pipes that blued in minutes and went rusty in hours. In the worst case they didn't even fit properly.

Yet in the 1970s and '80s, noisy, ill-fitting, performance-reducing exhausts were de rigueur. Not so in the classic world, so it's fortunate that complete pattern systems became available after Honda stepped aside. With a retail price of around £1,200 at the time of writing, these aren't cheap. Obviously, the state of the exhaust will have a significant influence on a four-pipe CB750's value.

The frame and suspension are straightforward enough. Check if anything is bent or out of line. And if the forks are leaking, it's quite likely that the stanchions are pitted, which costs rather more to fix than a pair of blown seals. Beware that after nearly half a century some frames will be rusting, internally or externally. This applies particularly to the swinging arm – all old Hondas tend to suffer here. If there's any doubt about its structural integrity, throw it away because sourcing a second-hand replacement should be easy enough.

External rust on chromed wheel rims and spokes is easy to spot, but the inside should also be checked on any bike that's being ridden. Obviously, this involves removing the tyres and tubes (which for safety's sake should also be thrown away if they're more than a few years old). Beware of crumbling inner rims around the spoke holes. Note also that peeling chrome is very sharp and could damage the tube, as can a rotten rim tape which exposes the sharp ends of spokes. While the wheels are off, inspect the brake shoes – the friction material can split, crack or detach itself from the shoe, which could jam the wheel.

Most CB750s have a rear drum, while F1 and later model owners only have disc calipers to worry about. The original swinging front caliper can be made to work reasonably well, but it's marginal by today's standards. The rotor won't give problems unless someone has drilled holes in it as a vain attempt to improve wet weather performance. The swinging caliper is perhaps not Honda's most famous hour, and seems to be the way it mainly avoids paying licence fees. If braking is poor and/or there's a squeal, either all the time or when applied, the problem is probably seizure of the pivoted arm bolted to the fork leg. Alternatively, the brake 'pucks' or hydraulic piston might be stuck in the caliper. Make sure everything is free-moving, and that the fixed pad is able to rock on its backing.

Moving onto the engine and transmission, this is where you can come unstuck. Firstly, if you're preparing to pay extra for an early 'sand-cast' model, make absolutely sure it is a sand-cast model, not an eclectic creation. Note, though, that as related earlier, the CB750 developed a reputation for jettisoning drive chains, which could and did smash the crankcases. If this happened they were replaced by the superior new smooth finish, pressure die-cast type, so does that count as non-standard?

Once out of warranty and demoted to the bargain banger end of market, cracked cases were sometimes repaired by welding, which might be difficult to spot under a coat of Honda's silver engine paint. No matter how skilful the work, welded alloy is likely to be weaker, but is a bike with repaired original rough crankcases, with a potentially major fault, worth more or less than one with later replacements that might have been there since 1971? To ride, or not to ride, that is the question.

Right: A linkage replaced cumbersome four-cable setup on K0 and later models. (Rod Ker)

Below: Tappet caps were often damaged by DIY-ers with the wrong tools. (Rod Ker)

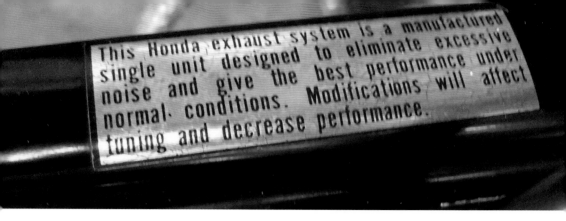

This Honda exhaust system is a manufactured single unit designed to eliminate excessive noise and give the best performance under normal conditions. Modifications will affect tuning and decrease performance.

Usually all too true! (Rod Ker)

Paying a substantial amount of money for any bike that is at least thirty-five years old is risky, of course – but not as risky as buying a non-runner. Be particularly wary of dismantled 'projects'. You might be able to ascertain that the main parts are present, but it's the small, less obvious bits and pieces that are difficult to find and expensive if/when you do. On the good news side, at least it will be easier to spot damaged crankcases.

If the restoration plan budgets for a complete engine rebuild, then the current state of the main, big end and camshaft journals and their bearing surfaces will be less crucial, but they will at least give a guide to the state of the rest of the engine internals. If the bike in question has been running on dirty oil (or air) expect everything to have suffered, including the primary and cam chains, tensioners, gears, bearings selector forks, etc. Remember that the Four not only has a dry sump, the gearbox is also lubricated by pumped oil.

One endemic Honda problem – due to amateur mechanics more than design faults – concerned the way the oil feed to the cams was routed up through passages in the head and barrels. It was all too easy for these channels to get blocked by debris (particularly instant gasket) or incorrect assembly. Depending on severity, this would result in seizure of the camshaft bearings, sometimes causing the cam to snap in two. Looking on the bright side, at least you could then limp home on a 368cc twin!

Another death by DIY involved forgetting to refit the metering jets leading to the cam bearings. In this scenario, plenty of oil would go upstairs but not enough to the bottom end. In any case, work on the engine usually involved removing it from the frame, because the top tubes just didn't leave enough space to remove the cylinder head. The motor had to be lifted out complete. Not the sort of thing you should try single-handed.

Apart from problems caused by it being such a tight fit in the frame, Japanese motorcycle restorers are finding that a few decades of 'electrolytic' corrosion can make engine bolts extremely difficult to remove. The same applies to cylinder head studs, unfortunately. Ironically, the CB750 often suffered top end oil leaks, which helped prevent seizures just as it does with incurably incontinent British machines! Honda's leaks usually involved failure to replace O-rings and gaskets, although there are also some often overlooked seals hidden underneath the cam carriers.

Another potential snag at decapitation time concerns the 6-mm bolts lurking inside the head. A slim socket will reach these, but that might not be much help if the heads are already rounded off by some oik trying to use a mangled box spanner. A face-drive 10-mm socket is the tool for the job. DIY dunces are also responsible for the typically butchered tappet covers. A full hexagon spanner is needed here, but there are conspiracy theorists who claim that Honda deliberately made the heads smaller than the nominal 17 mm so that it would be impossible to strip the threads, which would be much more expensive and involved to fix. The same logic applied to the 12 mm head oil filter retaining bolt. Aftermarket replacements have larger hexagons, but don't blame Mr H if you overtighten and destroy the lower crankcases.

Rest assured that CB750 engines are even more difficult to put back in the frame than they are to get out. In desperation, some mechanics have resorted to lying the frame on its side and then inserting the engine. Not a good idea, because it's easy to damage what's outboard of the crankshaft, either the sidecases or the ignition and alternator.

Drum rear brake: dependable and easy to fix. Watch out for crumbling linings, though. (Rod Ker)

Above: Curvaceous original exhausts: access to oil filter housing often restricted by aftermarket versions. (Rod Ker)

Left: Apart from the Japanese opposition, Italy's 1970s bike renaissance produced plenty of other models that made the Honda Four seem dull. (Rod Ker)

Based on the RCB double cam engine, the CB750KZ introduced in 1979 was a faster and more refined machine.

1969 *v.* the Twenty-First Century

The CB750 was a giant leap forward for motorcycling in 1969. Almost fifty years on, how does this iconic machine measure up to a current 'superbike'? Surprisingly well, is the short answer. Going back in time another half century, a bike produced just after the end of the First World War would seem to come from a different planet to the Four. To put it another way, a typical 1969 motorcyclist would be completely lost trying to start and operate a 1919 Triumph Single, for example, but anyone capable of riding today's bikes will have no trouble with an original CB750.

It could be argued that the Four and its later UJM imitators from Kawasaki, Suzuki and Yamaha were actually superior to succeeding no-compromise super sports bikes such as the Suzuki GSX-R750, which began to lose all pretence as practical everyday transport. In the 1980s the idea that a two-wheeler should be used for daily commuting was largely forgotten outside London. It's telling that in Britain new bike registrations peaked at over 300,000 in 1979, but sales then crashed and by 1986 the figure was less than 100,000, a level not seen since 1949.

After a tense period, the decline was arrested as motorcyclists returned to the fold and became obsessed with absolute performance, in the form of the 'race replica'. Carried along by a wave of older but not necessarily wiser RUBs (Rich Urban Bikers), all that apparently mattered was that this year's plastic rocket could circulate a racetrack slightly faster than last year's, even if that made it totally unsuitable for riding on normal public roads.

Plainly, there were flaws in such a sales strategy. Motorcyclists were a dying breed, far too literally, and all the world was not a 200 mph racetrack. As a result, we were in danger of disappearing up a blind alley or being legislated into oblivion. Luckily, a growing band of Captain Sensibles switched to cruisers and retros, effectively new bikes that looked like old bikes. Honda wasn't slow to exploit new niches, and in 1992 launched the CB Seven Fifty (that's what it was officially called, rather than CB750). Instead of sacrificing everything for speed, this tribute to the past was really a big softy.

More recently, Honda put much effort into the all-new CB1100 'modern classic', its first air-cooled Four for twenty years. Seen in prototype form in 2007 and on sale in some markets from 2010, it took another three years to decide that a European version should be produced. The intention was to create a homage to all the transverse-engined Fours of the

1970s and '80s, not just the CB750, but the main inspiration was obvious from its sloping air-cooled cylinders outwards.

In a shrinking market, only modest sales were expected, especially as the model was intended to be the sort of bike that would be bought and kept, not part-exchanged as soon as it went out of fashion. Selling something that doesn't need replacing is normally commercial suicide, but Honda must have its reasons.

Stepping off a new CB1100 ('A Motorcycle as Motorcycles Used to Be' ran the slogan) and straight onto its 1969 ancestor will initially be a slight culture shock because the oldie makes a lot more noise, both mechanical and exhaust. The transmission will also feel crude and clunky, and that famous front disc brake requires a determined squeeze to produce results. Beyond that not much has changed. The current 1140cc Four actually has a lower specific power output than the original, but delivered in a far more sophisticated manner, thanks to fuel injection. For all that, mpg figures are similar and the 88 bhp CB1100 isn't hugely faster.

Soichiro Honda firmly believed in development through new technology and engineering advancement. He therefore might not have approved of attempts to recreate the past, particularly features like asymmetric cam timing between banks of cylinders, purely to give the engine some olde worlde presence and character! Still, we can safely assume he was immensely proud to have his name on the first superbike.

The current CB1100 is a homage to all the fours of the 1970s. (Honda)

Specifications, 1969 model

Engine:
Air-cooled, four-cylinder, single overhead camshaft
Bore and stoke: 61 mm × 63 mm
Capacity: 736cc
Compression ratio: 9.0:1
Power: 67 bhp at 8,000 rpm
Torque: 44 lb/ft at 7,000 rpm
Carburettors: four Keihin 28 mm

Transmission:
Gearbox: five-speed constant mesh lubricated by oil pump
Ratios:
1st: 2.5:1
2nd: 1.708:1
3rd: 1.333:1
4th: 1.097:1
5th: 0.939:1
Primary drive: twin single-row chains
Primary reduction: 1.708:1
Secondary reduction: 1.167:1
Final reduction: 2.667:1 (18/48 teeth sprockets)

Chassis:
Welded steel twin cradle
Front suspension: oil damped fork, 5.6 inch travel
Rear suspension: oil damped coil springs, 3.3 inch travel

Brakes:
Front 290 mm (11.5 inch) disc, swinging single piston caliper
Rear single leading shoe 180 mm (7.1 inch) drum

Dimensions:
Length: 2,160 mm
Width: 885 mm
Height: 1,155 mm
Wheelbase: 1,455 mm
Seat height: 800 mm
Kerb weight: (see text) 235 kg (517 lb)

Wheels:
Spoked wire, chrome-plated steel rims

Tyres:

Front 3.25 × 19 inches
Rear 4.00 × 18 inches

Electrical:
12v negative earth
Ignition: twin contact breakers firing two cylinders using wasted spark system
Charging: 210 W three-phase alternator
Battery: 14 A/hr